1.   Indian Love Poetry – An Introduction

Love is a universal feeling but a few lines of musings from a poet – assembled words perhaps softly spoken - can express a romance or desire that if we don't yet have we'd probably like to. And so poets have burnished their dreams throughout history and across the globe, in every culture past and present.

For most of us Indian Love Poetry tends to be the erotic and explicit *Kama Sutra* and *The Perfumed Garden*.   Or the epic adventures in rather grander volumes such as The Epic Of Gilamesh or the Mahabararata.

But this Indian Love Poetry explores an altogether softer, gentler more soulful side.

Many of the poems you will hear are by writers now forgotten or obscure but whose words speak with a clarity and beauty that belies the fact they were written and translated, in some cases, many centuries ago from Sanskrit and Tamil and then later Hindi, Urdu, Malayalam and Bengali. This selection includes such famed poets as Tagore and Rumi who carefully document observed facets and flakes of love. Men speak about their love and longing for a woman and more unusually for its time, women speak of their love and longing for men. It's a special and unique compilation and whilst new and different is something we can still share and understand.

Indian Love Poetry is also available as an audiobook, read by Shyama Perera and Ghizela Rowe, and available at iTunes, Amazon and most digital stores.

2   Speak To Me, My Love!

Speak to me, my love! Tell me in words what you sang.
The night is dark. The stars are lost in clouds.
The wind is sighing through the leaves.
I will let loose my hair.
My blue cloak will cling round me like the night.
I will clasp your head to my bosom;
And there in the sweet loneliness murmur on your heart.
I will shut my eyes and listen.
I will not look in your face.
When your words are ended, we will sit still and silent.
Only the trees will whisper in the dark.
[The night will pale.] The day will dawn.
We shall look at each other's eyes and go on our different paths.
Speak to me, my love! Tell me in words what you sang.

~Rabindranath Tagore from 'The Gardener'

3   My Desire

Fate has given me many a gift
To which men most aspire,
Lovely, precious and costly things,
But not my heart's desire.

Many a man has a secret dream
Of where his soul would be,
Mine is a low verandah'd house
In a tope beside the sea.

Over the roof tall palms should wave,
Swaying from side to side,
Every night we should fall asleep
To the rhythm of the tide.

The dawn should be gay with song of birds,
And the stir of fluttering wings.
Surely the joy of life is hid
In simple and tender things!

At eve the waves would shimmer with gold
In the rosy sunset rays,
Emerald velvet flats of rice
Would rest the landward gaze.

A boat must rock at the laterite steps
In a reef-protected pool,
For we should sail through the starlit night
When the winds were calm and cool.

I am so tired of all this world,
Its folly and fret and care.
Find me a little scented home
Amongst thy loosened hair.

Give me a soft and secret place
Against thine amber breast,
Where, hidden away from all mankind,
My soul may come to rest.

Many a man has a secret dream
Of where his life might be;
Mine is a lovely, lonely place
With sunshine and the sea.

4   The Music Of Love

Hail to thee, then, O Love, sweet madness!
Thou who healest all our infirmities!
Who art the Physician of our pride and self-conceit!
Who art our Plato and our Galen!
Love exalts our earthly bodies to heaven,
And makes the very hills to dance with joy!
O lover, 'twas Love that gave life to Mount Sinai,
When "it quaked, and Moses fell down in a swoon."
Did my Beloved only touch me with His lips,
I too, like a flute, would burst out into melody.

5.   Song Of Ramesram, Temple Girl

Now is the season of my youth,
Not thus shall I always be,
Listen, dear Lord, thou too art young,
Take thy pleasure with me.
My hair is straight as the falling rain,
And fine as morning mist,
I am a rose awaiting thee
That none have touched or kissed.

Do as thou wilt with mine and me,
Beloved, I only pray,
Follow the promptings of thy youth.
Let there be no delay!

A leaf that flutters upon the bough,
A moment, and it is gone,--
A bubble amid the fountain spray,--
Ah, pause, and think thereon;
For such is youth and its passing bloom
That wait for thee this hour,
If aught in thy heart incline to me
Ah, stoop and pluck thy flower!

Come, my Lord, to the temple shade,
Where cooling fountains play,
If aught in thy heart incline to love
Let there be no delay!

Many shall faint with love of me
And I shall slake their thirst,
But Fate has brought thee hither to-day
That thou shouldst be the first.
Old, so old are the temple-walls,
Love is older than they;
But I am the short-lived temple rose,
Blooming for thee to-day.

Thine am I, Prince, and only thine,
What is there more so say ?
If aught in thy heart incline to love

6   The Kiss

Lips' language to lips' ears.
Two drinking each other's heart, it seems.
Two roving loves who have left home,
pilgrims to the confluence of lips.
Two waves rise by the law of love
to break and die on two sets of lips.
Two wild desires craving each other

meet at last at the body's limits.
Love's writing a song in dainty letters,
layers of kiss-calligraphy on lips.
Plucking flowers from two sets of lips
perhaps to thread them into a chain later.
This sweet union of lips
is the red marriage-bed of a pair of smiles.

7   The Rao Of Ilore

I was sold to the Rao of Ilore,
Slender and tall was he.
When his litter carried him down the street
I peeped through the thatch to see.
Ah, the eyes of the Rao of Ilore,
My lover that was to be!

The hair that lay on his youthful brow
Was curled like an ocean wave;
His eyes were lit with a tender smile,
But his lips were soft and grave.
For sake of these things I was still with joy
When the silver coins were paid,
And they took me up to the Palace gates,
Delighted and unafraid.
Ah, the eyes of the Rao of Ilore,
May never their brilliance fade!

So near was I to the crown of life!
Ten thousand times, alas!
The Diwan leant from the latticed hall,
Looked down and saw me pass.
He begged for me from the Rao of Ilore,
Who answered, "She is thine,
Thou wert ever more than a father to me,
And thy desires are mine."
Ah, the eyes of the Rao of Ilore
That never had looked in mine!

My years were spent in the Diwan's Courts,
My youth died down that day.
For sake of thine own content of mind
My lost beloved, I pray
That never my Lord a love may know
Like that he threw away.
Ah, the eyes of the Rao of Ilore,
Who threw my life away!

8   Song Of Songs

The love story of Krishna and Radha, which starts off badly when the God
starts to enjoy the pleasures of earth a little too much. This extract is a
bit of knowing tittle tattle about his seduction by nature and points to
later more serious seductions...

I know where Krishna tarries in these early days of Spring,
When every wind from warm Malay brings fragrance on its wing;
Brings fragrance stolen far away from thickets of the clove,
In jungles where the bees hum and the Koil flutes her love;
He dances with the dancers of a merry morrice one,
All in the budding Spring-time, for 'tis sad to be alone.

I know how Krishna passes these hours of blue and gold
When parted lovers sigh to meet and greet and closely hold
Hand fast in hand; and every branch upon the Vakul-tree
Droops downward with a hundred blooms, in every bloom a bee;
He is dancing with the dancers to a laughter-moving tone,
In the soft awakening Spring-time, when 'tis hard to live alone.

Where Kroona-flowers, that open at a lover's lightest tread,
Break, and, for shame at what they hear, from white blush modest red;
And all the spears on all the boughs of all the Ketuk-glades
Seem ready darts to pierce the hearts of wandering youths and maids;
Tis there thy Krishna dances till the merry drum is done,
All in the sunny Spring-time, when who can live alone?

Where the breaking forth of blossom on the yellow Keshra-sprays
Dazzles like Kama's sceptre, whom all the world obeys;
And Pâtal-buds fill drowsy bees from pink delicious bowls,
As Kama's nectared goblet steeps in languor human souls;
There he dances with the dancers, and of Radha thinketh none,
All in the warm new Spring-tide, when none will live alone.

Where the breath of waving Mâdhvi pours incense through the grove,
And silken Mogras lull the sense with essences of love,--
The silken-soft pale Mogra, whose perfume fine and faint
Can melt the coldness of a maid, the sternness of a saint--
There dances with those dancers thine other self, thine Own,
All in the languorous Spring-time, when none will live alone.

Where as if warm lips touched sealed eyes and waked them all the bloom
Opens upon the mangoes to feel the sunshine come;
And Atimuktas wind their arms of softest green about,
Clasping the stems, while calm and clear great Jumna spreadeth out;
There dances and there laughs thy Love, with damsels many an one,
In the rosy days of Spring-time, for he will not live alone.

9   The Bride

Beat on the Tom-toms, and scatter the flowers,
Jasmin, Hibiscus, vermillion and white,

This is the day, and the Hour of Hours,
Bring forth the Bride for her Lover's delight.
Maidens no more, as a maiden shall claim her,
Near, in his Mystery, draweth Desire.
Who, if she waver a moment, shall blame her?
She is a flower, and love is a fire.
Choti Tinchaurya syani hogayi!

Give her the anklets, the rings and the necklace,
Darken her eyelids with delicate Art,
Heighten the beauty, so youthful and fleckless,
By the Gods favoured, oh, Bridegroom thou art!
Twine in thy fingers her fingers so slender,
Circle together the Mystical Fire,
Bridegroom,--a whisper--be gentle and tender,
Choti Tinchaurya knows not desire.
Abhi Tinchaurya syani hogayi!

Bring forth the silks and the veil that shall cover
Beauty, till yesterday, careless and wild,
Red are her lips for the kiss of a lover,
Ripe are her breasts for the lips of a child.
Centre and Shrine of Mysterious Power,
Chalice of Pleasure and Rose of Delight,
Shyly aware of the swift-coming hour,
Waiting the shade and the silence of night,
Choti Tinchaurya syani hogayi!

Still must the Bridegroom his longing dissemble,
Longing to loosen the silk-woven cord,
Ah, how his fingers will flutter and tremble,
Fingers well skilled with the bridle and sword.
Thine is his valor oh, Bride, and his beauty,
Thine to possess and re-issue again,
Such is thy tender and passionate duty,
Licit thy pleasure and honoured thy pain.
Choti Tinchaurya syani hogayi!

Choti Tinchaurya, lovely and tender,
Still all unbroken to sorrow and strife.
Come to the Bridegroom who, silk-clad and slender,
Brings thee the Honour and Burden of Life.
Bidding farewell to thy light-hearted playtime,
Worship thy Lover with fear and delight,
Art thou not ever, though slave of his daytime,
Choti Tinchaurya, queen of his night?
Choti Tinchaurya syani hogayi!

10 The First Wife

Ah, my lord, are the tidings true,

That thy mother's jewels are shapen anew?

I hear that a bride has chosen been,
The stars consulted, the parents seen.

Had I been childless, had never there smiled
The brilliant eyes from the face of a child,

Then at least I had understood
This thing they tell me thou findest good.

But I have been down to the River of Death,
With painful footsteps and shuddering breath,

Seven times; thou hast daughters three,
And four young sons who are fair as thee.

I am not unlovely, over my head
Not twenty summers as yet have sped.

'T is eleven years since my opening life
Was given to thee by my father's wife.

Ah, those days--They were lovely to me,
When little and shy I waited for thee.

Till I locked my arms round my lover above,
A child in form but a woman in love.

And I bore thy sons, as a woman should,
Year by year, as is meet and good.

Thy mother was ever content with me--
And Oh, Beloved, I worshipped thee!

And now it's over; alas, my lord,
Better I felt thy sharpest sword.

I hear she is youthful and fair as I
When I came to thee in the days gone by.

Her breasts are firmer; this bosom slips
Somewhat, weighted by children's lips.

But they were thy children. Oh, lord my king,
Ah, why hast thy heart devised this thing ?

I am not as the women of this thy land,
Meek and timid, broken to hand.

From the distant North I was given to thee,
Whose daughters are passionate, fierce and free,

I could not dwell by a rival's side,
I seek a bridegroom, as thou a bride.

The night she yieldeth her youth to thee,
Death shall take his pleasure in me.

11.   Song of Songs II

The Penitence of Krishna: further into the epic poem, we find Radha
becoming anxious as Krishna's appreciation of the earthly inevitably
extends to those who people the earth: specifically the women, who
represent the fecundity of nature.

Ah, my Beloved! dancing those rash dances,
Ah, Minstrel! playing wrongful strains so well;
Ah, Krishna! Krishna with the honeyed lip!
Ah, Wanderer into foolish fellowship!
My Dancer, my Delight!--I love thee still.

O Dancer! strip thy peacock-crown away,
Rise! thou whose forehead is the star of day,
With beauty for its silver halo set;
Come! thou whose greatness gleams beneath its shroud
Like Indra's rainbow shining through the cloud--
Come, for I love thee, my Beloved! yet.

Must love thee--cannot choose but love thee ever,
My best Beloved--set on this endeavor,
To win thy tender heart and earnest eye
From lips but sadly sweet, from restless bosoms,
To mine, O Krishna with the mouth of blossoms!
To mine, thou soul of Krishna! yet I sigh

Half hopeless, thinking of myself forsaken,
And thee, dear Loiterer, in the wood o'ertaken
With passion for those bold and wanton ones,
Who knit thine arms as poison-plants gripe trees
With twining cords--their flowers the braveries
That flash in the green gloom, sparkling stars and stones.

My Prince! my Lotus-faced! my woe! my love!
Whose broad brow, with the tilka-spot above,
Shames the bright moon at full with fleck of cloud;
Thou to mistake so little for so much!
Thou, Krishna, to be palm to palm with such!
O Soul made for my joys, pure, perfect, proud!

Ah, my Beloved! in thy darkness dear;
Ah, Dancer! with the jewels in thine ear,
Swinging to music of a loveless love;

O my Beloved! in thy fall so high
That angels, sages, spirits of the sky
Linger about thee, watching in the grove.

I will be patient still, and draw thee ever,
My one Beloved, sitting by the river
Under the thick kadambas with that throng:
Will there not come an end to earthly madness?
Shall I not, past the sorrow, have the gladness?
Must not the love-light shine for him ere long?

12   Listen, Beloved

Listen, Beloved, the Casurinas quiver,
Each tassel prays the wind to set it free,
Hark to the frantic sobbing of the river,
Wild to attain extinction in the sea.
All Nature blindly struggles to dissolve
In other forms and forces, thus to solve
The painful riddle of identity.
Ah, that my soul might lose itself in thee!

Yet, my Beloved One, wherefore seek I union,
Since there is no such thing in all the world,
Are not our spirits linked in close communion,
And on my lips thy clinging lips are curled?
Thy tender arms are round my shoulders thrown,
I hear thy heart more loudly than my own,
And yet, to my despair, I know thee far,
As in the stellar darkness, star from star.

Even in times when love with bounteous measure
A simultaneous joy on us has shed,
In the last moment of delirious pleasure,
Ere the sense fail, or any force be fled,
My rapture has been even as a wall,
Shutting out any thought of thee at all!
My being, by its own delight possessed,
Forgot that it was sleeping on thy breast.

Ay, from his birth each man is vowed and given
To a vast loneliness, ungauged, unspanned,
Whether by pain and woe his soul be riven,
Or all fair pleasures clustered 'neath his hand.
His gain by day, his ecstasy by night,
His force, his folly, fierce or faint delight,
Suffering or sorrow, fortune, feud, or care,
Whate'er he find or feel, he may not share.

Lonely we join the world, and we depart
Even as lonely, having lived alone,

The breast that feeds us, the beloved one's heart,
The lips we kiss,--or curse--alike unknown.
Ay, even these lips of thine, so often kissed,
What certitude have I that they exist?
Alas, it is the truth, though harsh it seems,
I have been loved as sweetly in my dreams.

Therefore if I should seem too fiercely fond,
Too swift to love, too eager to attain,
Forgive the fervour that would forge beyond
The limits set to mortal joy and pain.
Knowing the soul's unmeasured loneliness,
My passion must be mingled with distress,
As I, despairing, struggle to draw near
What is as unattainable as dear.

Thirst may be quenched at any kindly river,
Rest may be found 'neath any arching tree.
No sleep allures, no draughts of love deliver
My spirit from its aching need of thee.
Thy sweet assentiveness to my demands,
All the caressive touches of thy hands,
These soft cool hands, with fingers tipped with fire,
They can do nothing to assuage desire.

Sometimes I think my longing soul remembers
A previous love to which it aims and strives,
As if this fire of ours were but the embers
Of some wild flame burnt out in former lives.
Perchance in earlier days I did attain
That which I seek for now so all in vain,
Maybe my soul with thine was fused and wed
In some great night, long since dissolved and dead.

We may progress; but who shall answer clearly
The riddle of the endless change of things.
Perchance in other days men loved more dearly,
Or Love himself had wider ways and wings,
Maybe we gave ourselves with less control,
Or simpler living left more free the soul,
So that with ease the flesh aside was flung,
Or was it merely that Mankind was young?

Or has my spirit a divine prevision
Of vast vague passions stored in days to be,
When some strong souls shall conquer their division
And two shall be as one, eternally?
Finding at last upon each other's breast,
Unutterable calm and infinite rest,
While love shall burn with such intense a glow
That both shall die, and neither heed or know.

Why do I question thus, and wake confusion
In the soft thought that lights thy perfect face,
Ah, shed once more thy perfumed hair's profusion,
Open thine arms and make my resting place.
Lay thy red lips on mine as heretofore,
Grant me the treasure of thy beauty's store,
Stifle all thought in one imperious kiss,
What shall I ask for more than this, and this?

13   Song Of Jasoda

Had I been young I could have claimed to fold thee
For many days against my eager breast;
But, as things are, how can I hope to hold thee
Once thou hast wakened from this fleeting rest?

Clear shone the moonlight, so that thou couldst find me,
Yet not so clear that thou couldst see my face,
Where in the shadow of the palms behind me
I waited for thy steps, for thy embrace.

What reck I now my morning life was lonely?
For widowed feet the ways are always rough.
Though thou hast come to me at sunset only,
Still thou hast come, my Lord, it is enough.

Ah, mine no more the glow of dawning beauty,
The fragrance and the dainty gloss of youth,
Worn by long years of solitude and duty,
I have no bloom to offer thee in truth.

Yet, since these eyes of mine have never wandered,
Still may they gleam with long forgotten light.
Since in no wanton way my youth was squandered,
Some sense of youth still clings to me tonight.

Thy lips are fresh as dew on budding roses,
The gold of dawn still lingers in thy hair,
While the abandonment of sleep discloses
How every attitude of youth is fair.

Thou art so pale, I hardly dare caress thee,
Too brown my fingers show against the white.
Ahi, the glory, that I should possess thee,
Ahi, the grief, but for a single night!

The tulip tree has pallid golden flowers
That grow more rosy as their petals fade;
Such is the splendour of my evening hours
Whose time of youth was wasted in the shade.

I shall not wait to see to-morrow's morning,
Too bright the golden dawn for me, too bright,
How could I bear thine eyes' unconscious scorning
Of what so pleased thee in the dimmer light?

It may be wine had brought some brief illusion,
Filling thy brain with rainbow fantasy,
Or youth, with moonlight, making sweet collusion,
Threw an alluring glamour over me

Therefore I leave thee softly, to awaken
When the first sun rays warm thy blue-veined breast,
Smiling and all unknowing I have taken
The poppied drink that brings me endless rest.

Thus would I have thee rise; thy fancy laden
With the vague sweetness of the bygone night,
Thinking of me as some consenting maiden,
Whose beauty blossomed first for thy delight.

While I, if any kindly visions hover
Around the silence of my last repose,
Shall dream of thee, my pale and radiant lover,
Who made my life so lovely at its close!

14   Song of Songs III

Later Krishna is again seduced by the beauty of the women he is meeting
on earth while Radha watches from above:

Something then of earth has held him
From his home above,
Some one of those slight deceivers
Ah, my foolish love!

Some new face, some winsome playmate,
With her hair untied,
And the blossoms tangled in it,
Woos him to her side.

On the dark orbs of her bosom
Passionately heaved
Sink and rise the warm, white pearl-strings,
Oh, my love deceived!

Fair? yes, yes! the rippled shadow
Of that midnight hair
Shows above her brow as clouds do
O'er the moon most fair:

And she knows, with wilful paces,

How to make her zone
Gleam and please him; and her ear-rings
Tinkle love; and grown

Coy as he grows fond, she meets him
With a modest show;
Shaming truth with truthful seeming,
While her laugh, light, low

And her subtle mouth that murmurs.
And her silken cheek,
And her eyes, say she dissembles
Plain as speech could speak.

Till at length, a fatal victress,
Of her triumph vain,
On his neck she lies and smiles there:
Ah, my Joy! My Pain!

15   Song of Songs IV

Follow, happy Radha! follow,
In the quiet falling twilight
The steps of him who followed thee
So steadfastly and far;
Let us bring thee where the banjulas
Have spread a roof of crimson,
Lit up by many a marriage-lamp
Of planet, sun, and star:
For the hours of doubt are over,
And thy glad and faithful lover
Hath found the road by tears and prayers
To thy divinest side;
And thou wilt not now deny him
One delight of all thy beauty,
But yield up open-hearted
His pearl, his prize, his bride.

Oh, follow! while we fill the air
With songs and softest music;
Lauding thy wedded loveliness,
Dear Mistress past compare!
For there is not any splendour
Of Apsarasas immortal
No glory of their beauty rich
But Radha has a share;
Oh, follow! while we sing the song
That fills the worlds with longing,
The music of the Lord of love
Who melts all hearts with bliss;
For now is born the gladness

That springs from mortal sadness,
And all soft thoughts and things and hopes
Were presages of this.

Then, follow, happiest Lady!
Follow him thou lovest wholly;
The hour is come to follow now
The soul thy spells have led;
His are thy breasts like jasper-cups,
And his thine eyes like planets;
Thy fragrant hair, thy stately neck,
Thy queenly sumptuous head;
Thy soft small feet, thy perfect lips,
Thy teeth like jasmine petals,
Thy gleaming rounded shoulders,
And long caressing arms,
Being thine to give, are his; and his
The twin strings of thy girdle,
And his the priceless treasure
Of thine utter-sweetest charms.

So follow! while the flowers break forth
In white and amber clusters,
At the breath of thy pure presence,
And the radiance on thy brow;
Oh, follow where the Asokas wave
Their sprays of gold and purple,
As if to beckon thee the way
That Krishna passed but now;
He is gone a little forward!
Though thy steps are faint for pleasure,
Let him hear the tattling ripple
Of the bangles round thy feet;
Moving slowly o'er the blossoms
On the path which he has shown thee,
That when he turns to listen
It may make his fond heart beat.

And loose thy jewelled girdle
A little, that its rubies
May tinkle softest music too,
And whisper thou art near;
Though now, if in the forest
Thou should'st bend one blade of Kusha
With silken touch of passing foot,
His heart would know and hear;
Would hear the wood-buds saying,
"It is Radha's foot that passes;"
Would hear the wind sigh love-sick,
"It is Radha's fragrance, this;"
Would hear thine own heart beating
Within thy panting bosom,

And know thee coming, coming,
His ever, ever his!

16   The Rice-boat

I slept upon the Rice-boat
That, reef protected, lay
At anchor, where the palm-trees
Infringe upon the bay.

The windless air was heavy
With cinnamon and rose,
The midnight calm seemed waiting,
Too fateful for repose.

One joined me on the Rice-boat
With wild and waving hair,
Whose vivid words and laughter
Awoke the silent air.

Oh, beauty, bare and shining,
Fresh washen in the bay,
One well may love by moonlight
What one would not love by day!

Above among the cordage
The night wind hardly stirred,
The lapping of the ripples
Was all the sound we heard.

Love reigned upon the Rice-boat,
And Peace controlled the sea,
The spirit's consolation,
The senses' ecstasy.

Though many things and mighty
Are furthered in the West,
The ancient Peace has vanished
Before To-day's unrest.

For how among their striving,
Their gold, their lust, their drink,
Shall men find time for dreaming
Or any space to think?

Think not I scorn the Science
That lightens human pain;
Though man's reliance often
Is placed on it in vain.

Maybe the long endeavour,

The patience and the strife,
May some day solve the riddle,
The Mystery of Life.

Perchance I do not value
Things Western as I ought,
The trains,--that take us, whither?
The ships,--that reach, what port?

To me it seems but chaos
Of greed and haste and rage,
The endless, aimless, motion
Of squirrels in a cage.

Here, where some ruined temple
In solitude decays,
With carven walls still hallowed
With prayers of bygone days,

Here, where the coral outcrops
Make "flowers of the sea,"
The olden Peace yet lingers,
In hushed serenity.

Ah, silent, silver moonlight,
Whose charm impartial falls
On tanks of sacred water
And squalid city walls,

Whose mystic whiteness hallows
The lowest and the least,
To thee men owe the glamour
That draws them to the East.

And as this azure water,
Unflecked by wave or foam,
Conceals in its tranquillity
The dreaded white shark's home,

So if love be illusion
I ask the dream to stay,
Content to love by moonlight
What I might not love by day.

17   The Lament Of Yasmini, The Dancing-Girl

Ah, what hast thou done with that Lover of mine?
The Lover who only cared for thee?
Mine for a handful of nights, and thine
For the Nights that Are and the Days to Be,

The scent of the Champa lost its sweet
So sweet is was in the Times that Were!
Since His alone, of the numerous feet
That climb my steps, have returned not there.
Ahi, Yasmini, return not there!

Art thou yet athrill at the touch of His hand,
Art thou still athirst for His waving hair?
Nay, passion thou never couldst understand,
Life's heights and depths thou wouldst never dare.

The Great Things left thee untouched, unmoved,
The Lesser Things had thy constant care.
Ah, what hast thou done with the Lover I loved,
Who found me wanting, and thee so fair?
Ahi, Yasmini, He found her fair!

Nay, nay, the greatest of all was thine;
The love of the One whom I craved for so,
But much I doubt if thou couldst divine
The Grace and Glory of Love, or know

The worth of the One whom thine arms embraced.
I may misjudge thee, but who can tell?
So hard it is, for the one displaced,
To weigh the worth of a rival's spell.
Ahi, Yasmini, thy rival's spell!

And Thou, whom I loved: have the seasons brought
That fair content, which allured Thee so?
Is it all that Thy delicate fancy wrought?
Yasmini wonders; she may not know.

Yet never the Stars desert the sky,
To fade away in the desolate Dawn,
But Yasmini watches their glory die,
And mourns for her own Bright Star withdrawn.
Ahi, Yasmini, the lonely dawn!

Ah, never the lingering gold dies down
In a sunset flare of resplendent light,
And never the palm-tree's feathery crown
Uprears itself to the shadowy night,

But Yasmini thinks of those evenings past,
When she prayed the glow of the glimmering West
To vanish quickly, that night, at last,
Might bring Thee back to her waiting breast.
Ahi, Yasmini, how sweet that rest!

Yet I would not say that I always weep;
The force, that made such a desperate thing

Of my love for Thee, has not fallen asleep,
The blood still leaps, and the senses sing,

While other passion has oft availed.
(Other Love--Ah, my One, forgive!)
To aid, when Churus and Opium failed;
I could not suffer so much and live.
Ahi, Yasmini, who had to live!

Nay, why should I say "Forgive" to Thee?
To whom my lovers and I are naught,
Who granted some passionate nights to me,
Then rose and left me with never a thought!

And yet, Ah, yet, for those Nights that Were,
Thy passive limbs and thy loose loved hair,
I would pay, as I have paid, all these days,
With the love that kills and the thought that slays.
Ahi, Yasmini, thy youth it slays!

The youthful widow, with shaven hair,
Whose senses ache for the love of a man,
The young Priest, knowing that women are fair,
Who stems his longing as best he can,

These suffer not as I suffer for Thee;
For the Soul desires what the senses crave,
There will never be pleasure or peace for me,
Since He who wounded, alone could save.
Ahi, Yasmini, He will not save!

The torchlight flares, and the lovers lean
Towards Yasmini, with yearning eyes,
Who dances, wondering what they mean,
And gives cold kisses, and scant replies.

They talk of Love, she withholds the name,
(Love came to her as a Flame of Fire!)
From things that are only a weary shame;
Trivial Vanity;--light Desire.
Ahi, Yasmini, the light Desire!

Yasmini bends to the praise of men,
And looks in the mirror, upon her hand,
To curse the beauty that failed her then
Ah, none of her lovers can understand!

How her whole life hung on that beauty's power,
The spell that waned at the final test,
The charm that paled in the vital hour,
Which won so many,--yet lost the best!
Ahi, Yasmini, who lost the best!

She leaves the dancing to reach the roof,
With the lover who claims the passing hour,
Her lips are his, but her eyes aloof
While the starlight falls in a silver shower.

Let him take what pleasure, what love, he may,
He, too, will suffer e'er life be spent,
But Yasmini's soul has wandered away
To join the Lover, who came, and went!
Ahi, Yasmini, He came, and went!

18   The Gardener

When She Passed Me By

When she passed by me with quick steps,
the end of her skirt touched me.
From the unknown island of a heart
came a sudden warm breath of spring.
A flutter of a flitting touch brushed me
and vanished in a moment,
like a torn flower petal blown in the breeze.
It fell upon my heart like a sigh of her body
and whisper of her heart.

Do Not Go My Love

Do not go, my love, without asking my leave.
I have watched all night,
and now my eyes are heavy with sleep;
I fear lest I lose you when I am sleeping.
Do not go, my love, without asking my leave.
I start up and stretch my hands to touch you.
I ask myself, "Is it a dream?"
Could I but entangle your feet with my heart,
And hold them fast to my breast!
Do not go, my love, without asking my leave

Your Questioning Eyes

Your questioning eyes are sad. They seek to know my
meaning as the moon would fathom the sea.
I have bared my life before your eyes from end to end,
with nothing hidden or held back.
That is why you know me not.
If it were only a gem, I could break it into a hundred
pieces and string them into a chain to put on your neck.
If it were only a flower, round and small and sweet, I could
pluck it from its stem to set it in your hair.
But it is a heart, my beloved.

Where are its shores and its bottom?

You know not the limits of this kingdom,
still you are its queen.
If it were only a moment of pleasure it would flower in an
easy smile, and you could see it and read it in a moment.
If it were merely a pain it would melt in limpid tears,
reflecting its inmost secret without a word.
But it is love, my beloved.
Its pleasure and pain are boundless,
and endless its wants and wealth.
It is as near to you as your life,
but you can never wholly know it.

19   The Net Of Memory

I cast the Net of Memory,
Man's torment and delight,
Over the level Sands of Youth
That lay serenely bright,
Their tranquil gold at times submerged
In the Spring Tides of Love's Delight.

The Net brought up, in silver gleams,
Forgotten truth and fancies fair:
Like opal shells, small happy facts
Within the Net entangled were
With the red coral of his lips,
The waving seaweed of his hair.

We were so young; he was so fair.

20   Oh, Unforgotten And Only Lover

Oh, unforgotten and only lover,
Many years have swept us apart,
But none of the long dividing seasons
Slay your memory in my heart.
In the clash and clamour of things unlovely
My thoughts drift back to the times that were,
When I, possessing thy pale perfection,
Kissed the eyes and caressed the hair.

Other passions and loves have drifted
Over this wandering, restless soul,
Rudderless, chartless, floating always
With some new current of chance control.
But thine image is clear in the whirling waters--
Ah, forgive--that I drag it there,
For it is so part of my very being

That where I wander it too must fare.

Ah, I have given thee strange companions,
To thee--so slender and chaste and cool--
But a white star loses no glimmer of beauty
In all the mud of a miry pool
That holds the grace of its white reflection;
Nothing could fleck thee, nothing could stain,
Thou hast made a home for thy delicate beauty
Where all things peaceful and lovely reign.

Doubtless the night that my soul remembers
Was a sin to thee, and thine only one.
Thou thinkest of it, if thou thinkest ever,
As a crime committed, a deed ill done.
But for me, the broken, the desert-dweller,
Following Life through its underways,--
I know if those midnights thou hadst not granted
I had not lived through these after days.

And that had been well for me; all would say so,
What have I done since I parted from thee?
But things that are wasted, and full of ruin,
All unworthy, even of me.
Yet, it was to me that the gift was given,
No greater joy have the Gods above,--
That night of nights when my only lover,
Though all reluctant, granted me love.

For thy beauty was mine, and my spirit knows it,
Never, ah, never my heart forgets,
One thing fixed, in the torrent of changing,
Faults and follies and fierce regrets.
Thine eyes and thy hair, that were lovely symbols
Of that white soul that their grace enshrined,
They are part of me and my life for ever,
In every fibre and cell entwined.

Men might argue that having known thee
I had grown faithful and pure as thee,
Had turned at the touch of thy grace and glory
From the average pathways trodden by me.
Hadst thou been kinder or I been stronger
It may be even these things had been--
But one thing is clear to my soul for ever,
I owe my owning of thee to sin.

Had I been colder I had not reached thee,
Besmirched the ermine, beflecked the snow
It was only sheer and desperate passion
That won thy beauty in years ago.
And not for the highest virtues in Heaven,

The utmost grace that the soul can name,
Would I resign what the sin has brought me,
Which I hold glory, and thou thy shame.

I talk of sin in the usual fashion,
But God knows what is a sin to me
We love more fiercely or love more faintly
But I doubt if it matters how these things be.
The best and the worst of us all sink under
What I held passion and thou held'st lust
What name will it find in a few more seasons,
When we both dissolve in an equal dust?

If a God there be, and a God seems needed
To make the beauty of things like thee,
He doubtless also, some careless moment,
Mixed the forces that fashioned me.
Also He, for His own good reason
Though I care little how these things are
Gave me thee, in those few brief midnights,
And that one solace He never can mar.

Ah me, the stars of such varying heavens
Have watched me, under such alien skies,
Lay thy beauty naked before me
To soothe and solace my world-worn eyes.
For one good gift to me has been given
A memory accurate, clear and keen,
That holds the vision, perfect for ever
In charm and glory, of things once seen.

So I hold thee there, and my fancy wanders
To each known beauty and blue-veined place,
I know how each separate eyelash trembles,
And every shadow that sweeps thy face.
And this is a joy of which none can rob me,
This is a pleasure that none can mar
As sweet as thou wert, in that long past midnight,
Even as lovely my memories are.

Ah, unforgotten and only lover,
If ever I drift across thy thought,
As even a vision unloved, unlovely,
May cross the fancy, uncalled, unsought,
When the years that pass thee have shown, in passing,
That my love, in its strength at least, was rare
Wilt thou not think--ah, hope of the hopeless
E'en as thou wouldst not, thou wilt not care!

21   Yasin Khan

Ay, thou has found thy kingdom, Yasin Khan,
Thy fathers' pomp and power are thine, at last.
No more the rugged roads of Khorasan,
The scanty food and tentage of the past!

Wouldst thou make war? thy followers know no fear.
Where shouldst thou lead them but to victory?
Wouldst thou have love? thy soft-eyed slaves draw near,
Eager to drain thy strength away from thee.

My thoughts drag backwards to forgotten days,
To scenes etched deeply on my heart by pain;
The thirsty marches, ambuscades, and frays,
The hostile hills, the burnt and barren plain.

Hast thou forgotten how one night was spent,
Crouched in a camel's carcase by the road,
Along which Akbar's soldiers, scouting, went,
And he himself, all unsuspecting, rode?

Did we not waken one despairing dawn,
Attacked in front, cut off in rear, by snow,
Till, like a tiger leaping on a fawn,
Half of the hill crashed down upon the foe?

Once, as thou mournd'st thy lifeless brother's fate,
The red tears falling from thy shattered wrist,
A spent Waziri, forceful still, in hate,
Covered they heart, ten paces off, and missed!

Ahi, men thrust a worn and dinted sword
Into a velvet-scabbarded repose;
The gilded pageants that salute thee Lord
Cover one sorrow-rusted heart, God knows.

Ah, to exchange this wealth of idle days
For one cold reckless night of Khorasan!
To crouch once more before the camp-fire blaze
That lit the lonely eyes of Yasin Khan.

To watch the starlight glitter on the snows,
The plain stretched round us like a waveless sea,
Waiting until thy weary lids should close
To slip my furs and spread them over thee.

How the wind howled about the lonely pass,
While the faint snow-shine of that plateaued space
Lit, where it lay upon the frozen grass,
The mournful, tragic beauty of thy face.

Thou hast enough caressed the scented hair
Of these soft-breasted girls who waste thee so.

Hast thou not sons for every adult year?
Let us arise, O Yasin Khan, and go!

Let us escape from these prison bars
To gain the freedom of an open sky,
Thy soul and mine, alone beneath the stars,
Intriguing danger, as in days gone by.

Nay; there is no returning, Yasin Khan.
The white peaks ward the passes, as of yore,
The wind sweeps o'er the wastes of Khorasan;
But thou and I go thitherward no more.

Close, ah, too close, the bitter knowledge clings,
We may not follow where my fancies yearn.
The years go hence, and wild and lovely things,
Their own, go with them, never to return.

22   On The Nature Of Love

The night is black and the forest has no end;
a million people thread it in a million ways.
We have trysts to keep in the darkness, but where
or with whom - of that we are unaware.
But we have this faith - that a lifetime's bliss
will appear any minute, with a smile upon its lips.
Scents, touches, sounds, snatches of songs
brush us, pass us, give us delightful shocks.
Then peradventure there's a flash of lightning:
whomever I see that instant I fall in love with.
I call that person and cry: `This life is blest!
for your sake such miles have I traversed!'
All those others who came close and moved off
in the darkness - I don't know if they exist or not.

23   Ashore

Out I came from the dancing-place:
The night-wind met me face to face

A wind off the harbour, cold and keen,
"I know," it whistled, "where thou hast been."

A faint voice fell from the stars above
"Thou? whom we lighted to shrines of Love!"

I found when I reached my lonely room
A faint sweet scent in the unlit gloom.

And this was the worst of all to bear,

For someone had left while lilac there.

The flower you loved, in times that were.

24   Lover's Gifts I

Come To My Garden Walk

Come to my garden walk, my love. Pass by the fervid flowers that
press themselves on your sight. Pass them by, stopping at some
chance joy, which like a sudden wonder of sunset illumines, yet
elude.
For lover's gift is shy, it never tells its name, it flits
across the shade, spreading a shiver of joy along the dust.
Overtake it or miss it for ever. But a gift that can be
grasped is merely a frail flower, or a lamp with flame that will
flicker.

Lover's Gifts - She Is Near to My Heart

She is near to my heart as the meadow-flower to the earth; she is
sweet to me as sleep is to tired limbs. My love for her is my life
flowing in its fullness, like a river in autumn flood, running with
serene abandonment. My songs are one with my love, like the murmur
of a stream, that sings with all its waves and current.

Lover's Gifts - In The Beginning Of Time

In the beginning of time, there rose from the churning of God's
dream two women. One is the dancer at the court of paradise, the
desired of men, she who laughs and plucks the minds of the wise
from their cold meditations and of fools from their emptiness; and
scatters them like seeds with careless hands in the extravagant
winds of March, in the flowering frenzy of May.
The other is the crowned queen of heaven, the mother, throned
on the fullness of golden autumn; she who in the harvest-time
brings straying hearts to the smile sweet as tears, the beauty deep
as the sea of silence, -brings them to the temple of the Unknown,
at the holy confluence of Life and Death.

Lover's Gifts - I Would Ask For Still More

I would ask for still more, if I had the sky with all its stars,
and the world with its endless riches; but I would be content with
the smallest corner of this earth if only she were mine.

Lover's Gifts - Last Night In The Garden

Last night in the garden I offered you my youth's foaming wine. You
lifted the cup to your lips, you shut your eyes and smiled while
I raised your veil, unbound your tresses, drawing down upon my
breast your face sweet with its silence, last night when the moon's
dream overflowed the world of slumber.
To-day in the dew-cooled calm of the dawn you are walking to
God's temple, bathed and robed in white, with a basketful of
flowers in your hand. I stand aside in the shade under the tree,
with my head bent, in the calm of the dawn by the lonely road to
the temple.

25   Written In Cananore

Who was it held that Love was soothing or sweet?
Mine is a painful fire, at its whitest heat.

Who said that Beauty was ever a gentle joy?
Thine is a sword that flashes but to destroy.

Though mine eyes rose up from thy Beauty's banquet, calm and
refreshed,
My lips, that were granted naught, can find no rest.

My soul was linked with thine, through speech and silent hours,
As the sound of two soft flutes combined, or the scent of sister flowers.

But the body, that wretched slave of the Sultan, Mind,
Who follows his master ever, but far behind,

Nothing was granted him, and every rebellious cell
Rises up with angry protest, "It is not well!

Night is falling; thou hast departed; I am alone;
And the Last Sweetness of Love thou hast not given - I have not known!"

Somewhere, Oh, My Beloved One, the house is standing,
Waiting for thee and me; for our first caresses.

It may be a river-boat, or a wave-washed landing,
The shade of a tree in the jungle's dim recesses,

Some far-off mountain tent, ill-pitched and lonely,
Or the naked vault of the purple heavens only.

But the Place is waiting there; till the Hour shall show it,
And our footsteps, following Fate, find it and know it.

Where we shall worship the greatest of all the Gods in his pomp and
power,
I sometimes think that I shall not care to survive that hour!

26   Lover's Gifts II: Are You A Mere Picture

Are you a mere picture, and not as true as those stars, true as
this dust? They throb with the pulse of things, but you are
immensely aloof in your stillness, painted form.
The day was when you walked with me, your breath warm, your
limbs singing of life. My world found its speech in your voice, and
touched my heart with your face. You suddenly stopped in your walk,
in the shadow-side of the Forever, and I went on alone.
Life, like a child, laughs, shaking its rattle of death as it
runs; it beckons me on, I follow the unseen; but you stand there,
where you stopped behind that dust and those stars; and you are a
mere picture.
No, it cannot be. Had the life-flood utterly stopped in you,
it would stop the river in its flow, and the foot-fall of dawn in
her cadence of colours. Had the glimmering dusk of your hair
vanished in the hopeless dark, the woodland shade of summer would die
with its dreams.
Can it be true that I forgot you? We haste on without heed,
forgetting the flowers on the roadside hedge. Yet they breathe
unaware into our forgetfulness, filling it with music. You have
moved from my world, to take seat at the root of my life, and
therefore is this forgetting-remembrance lost in its own depth.
You are no longer before my songs, but one with them. You came
to me with the first ray of dawn. I lost you with the last gold of
evening. Ever since I am always finding you through the dark. No,
you are no mere picture.

Lover's Gifts - Dying, You Have Left Behind

Dying, you have left behind you the great sadness of the Eternal
in my life. You have painted my thought's horizon with the sunset
colours of your departure, leaving a track of tears across the
earth to love's heaven. Clasped in your dear arms, life and death
united in me in a marriage bond.
I think I can see you watching there in the balcony with your
lamp lighted, where the end and the beginning of all things meet.
My world went hence through the doors that you opened-you holding
the cup of death to my lips, filling it with life from your own.

Lover's Gifts - I Dreamt

I dreamt that she sat by my head, tenderly ruffling my hair with
her fingers, playing the melody of her touch. I looked at her face
and struggled with my tears, till the agony of unspoken words burst
my sleep like a bubble.
I sat up and saw the glow of the Milky Way above my window,
like a world of silence on fire, and I wondered if at this moment
she had a dream that rhymed with mine

Lover's Gifts - She Dwelt Here by the Pool

She dwelt here by the pool with its landing-stairs in ruins. Many
an evening she had watched the moon made dizzy by the shaking of
bamboo leaves, and on many a rainy day the smell of the wet earth
had come to her over the young shoots of rice.
Her pet name is known here among those date-palm groves and
in the courtyards where girls sit and talk while stitching their
winter quilts. The water in this pool keeps in its depth the memory
of her swimming limbs, and her wet feet had left their marks, day
after day, on the footpath leading to the village.
The women who come to-day with their vessels to the water have
all seen her smile over simple jests, and the old peasant, taking
his bullocks to their bath, used to stop at her door every day to
greet her.
Many a sailing-boat passes by this village; many a traveller
takes rest beneath that banyan tree; the ferry-boat crosses to
yonder ford carrying crowds to the market; but they never notice
this spot by the village road, near the pool with its ruined
landing-stairs,-where dwelt she whom I love.

Lover's Gifts XVIII: Your Days

Your days will be full of cares, if you must give me your heart.
My house by the cross-roads has its doors open and my mind is
absent, -for I sing.
I shall never be made to answer for it, if you must give me
your heart. If I pledge my word to you in tunes now, and am too
much in earnest to keep it when music is silent, you must forgive
me; for the law laid down in May is best broken in December.
Do not always keep remembering it, if you must give me your
heart. When your eyes sing with love, and your voice ripples with
laughter, my answers to your questions will be wild, and not
miserly accurate in facts, -they are to be believed for ever and
then forgotten for good.

27   The Tom-Toms

Dost thou hear the tom-toms throbbing,
Like a lonely lover sobbing
For the beauty that is robbing him of all his life's delight?
Plaintive sounds, restrained, enthralling,
Seeking through the twilight falling
Something lost beyond recalling, in the darkness of the night.

Oh, my little, loved Firoza,
Come and nestle to me closer,
Where the golden-balled Mimosa makes a canopy above,
For the day, so hot and burning,
Dies away, and night, returning,

Sets thy lover's spirit yearning for thy beauty and thy love.

Soon will come the rosy warning
Of the bright relentless morning,
When, thy soft caresses scorning, I shall leave thee in the shade.
All the day my work must chain me,
And its weary bonds restrain me,
For I may not re-attain thee till the light begins to fade.

But at length the long day endeth,
As the cool of night descendeth
His last strength thy lover spendeth in returning to thy breast,
Where beneath the Babul nightly,
While the planets shimmer whitely,
And the fire-flies glimmer brightly, thou shalt give him love and rest.

Far away, across the distance,
The quick-throbbing drums' persistence
Shall resound, with soft insistence, in the pauses of delight,
Through the sequence of the hours,
While the starlight and the flowers
Consecrate this love of ours, in the Temple of the Night.

28   Lallji My Desire

"This is no time for saying 'no'"
Were thy last words to me,
And yet my lips refused the kiss
They might have given thee.
How could I know
That thou wouldst go
To sleep so far from me?

They took thee to the Burning-Ghat,
Oh, Lallji, my desire,
And now a faint and lonely flame
Uprises from the pyre.
The thin grey smoke in spirals drifts
Across the opal sky.
Would that I were a wife of thine,
And thus with thee could die!
How could I know
That thou wouldst go,
Oh, Lallji, my desire?
The lips I missed
The flames have kissed
Upon the Sandal pyre.

If one should meet me with a knife
And cut my heart in twain,
Then would he see the smoke arise

From every severed vein.
Such is the burning, inward fire,
The anguish of my pain,
For my Beloved, whose dying lips
Implored a kiss in vain!
How could I know
That thou wouldst go,
Oh, Lallji, my desire?
Too young thou art
To lay thy heart
Upon the Sandal pyre.

Thy wife awaits her coming child;
What were a child to me,
If I might take thee in these arms
And face the flames with thee?
The priests are chanting round the pyre,
At dusk they will depart
And leave to thee thy lonely rest,
To me my lonelier heart.
How could I know
Thou lovedst me so?
Upon the Sandal pyre
He lies forsaken.
The flames have taken
My Lallji, my desire!

29   Though In My Firmament Thou Wilt Not Shine

Talk not, my Lord, of unrequited love,
Since love requites itself most royally.
Do we not live but by the sun above,
And takes he any heed of thee or me?

Though in my firmament thou wilt not shine,
Thy glory, as a Star, is none the less.
Oh, Rose, though all unplucked by hand of mine,
Still am I debtor to thy loveliness.

Let there be no delay!

30   The Flame Of Love

How long wilt thou dwell on words and empty shows?
A burning heart is what I want; consort with burning!
Kindle in thy heart the flame of Love,
And burn up utterly thoughts and fine expressions.
O Moses! the lovers of fair rites are one class,
They whose hearts and souls burn with Love, another.

31   Song Of The Peri

Beauty, the Gift of Gifts, I give to thee.
Pleasure and love shall spring around thy feet
As through the lake the lotuses arise
Pinkly transparent and divinely sweet.

I give thee eyes aglow like morning stars,
Delicate brows, a mist of sable tresses,
That all the journey of thy lie may be
Lit up by love and softened by caresses.

For those who once were proud and softly bred
Shall, kneeling, wait thee as thou passest by,
They who were pure shall stretch forth eager hands
Crying, "Thy pity, Lord, before we die!"

And one shall murmur, "If the sun at dawn
Shall open and caress a happy flower,
What blame to him, although the blossom fade
In the full splendour of his noontide power?"

And one, "If aloes close together grow
It may well chance a plant shall wounded be,
Pierced by the thorn tips of another's leaves,
Thus am I hurt unconsciously by thee."

For some shall die and many more shall sin,
Suffering for thy sake till seven times seven,
Because of those most perfect lips of thine
Which held the power to make or mar their heaven.

And though thou givest back but cruelty,
Their love, persistent, shall not heed nor care,
All those whose ears are fed with blame of thee
Shall say, "It may be so, but he was fair."

Ay, those who lost the whole of youth for thee,
Made early and for ever, shamed and sad,
Shall sigh, re-living some sweet memory,
"Ah, once it was his will to make me glad."

Thy nights shall be as bright as summer days,
The sequence of thy sins shall seem as duty,
Since I have given thee, Oh, Gift of Gifts!--
The pale perfection of unrivalled beauty.

32   Shivratri (The Night Of Shiva)

(While the procession passed at Ramesram)

Nearer and nearer cometh the car
Where the Golden Goddess towers,
Sweeter and sweeter grows the air
From a thousand trampled flowers.
We two rest in the Temple shade
Safe from the pilgrim flood,
This path of the Gods in olden days
Ran royally red with blood.

Louder and louder and louder yet
Throbs the sorrowful drum
That is the tortured world's despair,
Never a moment dumb.
Shriller and shriller shriek the flutes,
Nature's passionate need
Paler and paler grow my lips,
And still thou bid'st them bleed.

Deeper and deeper and deeper still,
Never a pause for pain
Darker and darker falls the night
That golden torches stain.
Closer, ah! closer, and still more close,
Till thy soul reach my soul
Further, further, out on the tide
From the shores of self-control.

Glowing, glowing, to whitest heat,
Thy feverish passions burn,
Fiercer and fiercer, cruelly fierce,
To thee my senses yearn.
Fainter and fainter runs my blood
With desperate fight for breath
This, my Beloved, thou sayest is Love,
Or I should have deemed it Death!

33   Unending Love

I seem to have loved you in numberless forms, numberless times
In life after life, in age after age, forever.
My spellbound heart has made and remade the necklace of songs,
That you take as a gift, wear round your neck in your many forms,
In life after life, in age after age, forever.

Whenever I hear old chronicles of love, it's age old pain,
It's ancient tale of being apart or together.
As I stare on and on into the past, in the end you emerge,
Clad in the light of a pole-star, piercing the darkness of time.
You become an image of what is remembered forever.

You and I have floated here on the stream that brings from the fount.
At the heart of time, love of one for another.
We have played along side millions of lovers,
Shared in the same shy sweetness of meeting,
the distressful tears of farewell,
Old love but in shapes that renew and renew forever.